Daily Character Education Activities

Grades 2–3

by Becky Daniel-White

Carson-Dellosa Publishing Company, Inc.
Greensboro, North Carolina

Credits

Editor
Sabena Maiden

Cover Design
Peggy Jackson

Cover Photo
© Digital Vision® Ltd.
All rights reserved

Layout Design
Jon Nawrocik

Inside Illustrations
Jenny Campbell

ISBN 0-88724-206-5

Table of Contents

Table of Contents

What a big task you have set before yourself! Not only are you concerned about teaching your students the required academic curriculum, but you have also decided to take on the awesome, daily responsibility of helping your students become responsible, caring citizens.

This book of 180 activities—something for each day of the school year—is designed to make character building a positive and beneficial experience for you and your students. The book is organized into 10 chapters, one for each character trait: citizenship, compassion, fairness, honesty, integrity, perseverance, responsibility, respect, self-discipline, and trustworthiness. Each character trait chapter has daily activities designed to be used for three or four weeks.

To strengthen the home-school connection and show how important it is for families to reinforce good character at home, there is a reproducible parent letter at the beginning of each chapter. This helps keep parents and guardians informed and lets them know the Wednesday assignments, which the adults will help their children complete. The goal is for these real-world applications to help students comprehend the concept on a personal level, as well as give parents the opportunities to support and be informed about the classroom character lessons.

The weekly format of activities is consistent throughout the book. On Mondays, get off to a good start with *Check It Out!* lessons. These thought-provoking lessons will introduce the basic concept through popular children's stories, rhymes, or open conversation often with follow-up discussion questions. (Note that the children's stories selected are taken from popular children's books that you or your school library probably have or that are available for check-out at the local library.) Tuesdays' activities are called *Try It Out!* These projects and tasks will give students opportunities to demonstrate that they comprehend the topic. Wednesdays' *Take It Out!* lessons are short activities that are often directly related to the take-home assignments that students can share with parents. Each Thursday, students will *Talk It Out!* After sharing what they discussed with their parents the night before, students are able to transfer what they heard at home which will reinforce what they are discovering about themselves in the classroom. Fridays' *Act It Out!* activities are suggestions for role plays, games, puppet plays, and other active strategies to culminate each week's study. This gives students opportunities to demonstrate their understanding of the traits.

Also, the theme song "If You Have Character and You Know It" is provided on each parent letter with the new verse featuring that chapter's character trait. (See page 64 for the complete song.) This song can be sung in class at the beginning of each week to get students focused on the trait and as a closing activity after Fridays' *Act It Out!* lessons.

If you teach students that they are responsible for their own characters and that their daily choices determine who they are, then you have succeeded in your goal—making your students better people.

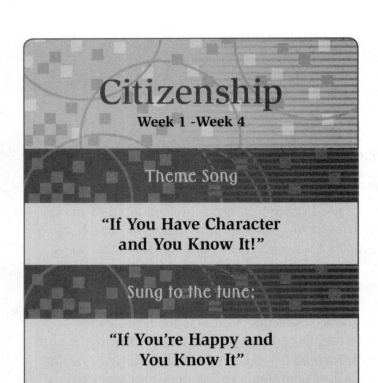

Citizenship
Week 1 - Week 4

Theme Song

"If You Have Character and You Know It!"

Sung to the tune:

"If You're Happy and You Know It"

■ ■ ■ ■ ■ ■ ■

Verse 1:
A good citizen loves the earth—
   yes sir-eee!
A good citizen loves the earth—
   yes sir-eee!
Take care of everything that breathes,
People, pets, and even trees,
A good citizen loves the earth—
   yes sir-eee!

Repeated Verse:
If you have character and you know
   it—let it show!
If you have character and you know
   it—let it show!
In everything along your way,
In all you do and say,
If you have character and you know
   it—let it show!

Dear Parents and Guardians,

For the next four weeks, our class will be exploring ways of demonstrating good citizenship. We will be singing our theme song, "If You Have Character and You Know It," including the verse about being a good citizen. We will be adding to the song each week. Please sing the song at home with your child.

On Wednesdays, your child will bring home a question or activity to be completed with your help. This week's assignments are listed below.

Week One: Your child will ask you what you think are the three most important qualities of a good friend.

Week Two: Your child will ask you what you think is the most important part of nature and why.

Week Three: Your child will share an animal picture with you. Please help your child label the animal's main parts (such as head, eyes, body, legs, and feet).

Week Four: Your child will ask you to help him or her complete the "I Can Be a Good Citizen" worksheet.

Daily Character Education • CD-0066 • © Carson-Dellosa

Citizenship

Be a Good Citizen by Being a Good Friend

Objective: Students will learn that being a friend is the beginning of understanding citizenship.

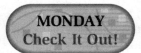

MONDAY
Check It Out!

Read aloud the fable "The Goatherd and the Wild Goats."

One day, some wild goats got mixed among a herder's goats. Thinking he might add them to his herd, the goatherd locked them up with his other animals. The next day, the man gave his own goats only a little food. Hoping that he could make the wild goats want to stay with his herd, he fed them abundantly each day. After a week, when he led the goats to pasture, the wild goats scampered off. The goatherd ran after them scolding, "Ungrateful goats! I took care of you better than my own goats, but still you scamper off."

One of the wild goats bleated back at him, "That is why we leave. Since you treated us better than your own goats, we know that when other goats come along, you will prefer them to us." —Aesop

Discussion Questions:
1. Do you think the wild goat was right with its prediction?
2. Do you treat new friends more kindly than you do your old friends?
3. What are some things that a friend does to let you know he is loyal?
4. How do you select friends?
5. How do you keep good friends?

TUESDAY
Try It Out!

Have students brainstorm ways that they can be good friends. List all of their ideas on the board. Then, create a recipe for friendship. Write the recipe on poster board to display as a reminder of the ingredients of good friendship.

For example: Mix the following ingredients together for a sweet friendship:
1 cup of patience   a generous helping of listening
2-3 hugs per day   1 giant scoop of kindness
13 big smiles per day   sprinkle with sugar and spice

WEDNESDAY
Take It Out!

Provide students with copies of "A Question of Friends." (See page 8.) Explain that a good way to make friends is to ask questions in order to learn about each other. Play this game in class to show students the potential friends they have at school.

Take-Home Activity: Have students ask their parents what they think are the three most important qualities of a good friend.

THURSDAY
Talk It Out!

During group time, have students share what their parents said are the qualities of a good friend. List the qualities on the board. Ask students to think about which of those qualities they show to their friends.

FRIDAY
Act It Out!

Divide the class into pairs. Have each pair role-play this situation: One child is new in your class; the other has been a student at the school since kindergarten. Have students take turns being the new student and the other student who helps her feel welcomed.

End the activity by singing "If You Have Character and You Know It."

A Question of Friends

Find someone who can answer "yes" to a question on the list and ask him or her to write or sign his or her name on the appropriate line. Try to collect as many signatures as possible. The same person should not sign the sheet more than twice.

Name _____

1. Is your favorite color blue? _____

2. Do you have an "n" in your full name? _____

3. Do you live in a white house? _____

4. Is your favorite day Saturday? _____

5. Do you have a pet bird or hamster? _____

6. Does your mom or dad drive a black car? _____

7. Is the beginning of your phone number _ _ _ (yours)? _____

8. Is your favorite season winter? _____

9. Do you know all of the words to the national anthem? _____

10. Do you have a grandparent living in our state? _____

11. Can you ice-skate? _____

12. Do you play a musical instrument? _____

13. Is your favorite drink orange juice? _____

14. Do you like playing sports? _____

15. Are you left-handed? _____

Citizenship

Be a Good Citizen by Appreciating Nature

Objective: Students will learn that being a good citizen means appreciating nature around them.

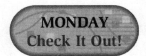
MONDAY
Check It Out!

Read aloud the book *The Giving Tree* by Shel Silverstein (HarperCollins Juvenile Books, 1964). A boy learns from a tree that he has been given much by nature.

Discussion Questions:
1. Why do you think the tree was so giving to the boy?
2. What things did the tree give the boy?
3. What kinds of things do real plants provide us?
4. What other things in nature provide for humans?
5. What can you do to help plants and other parts of nature?

TUESDAY
Try It Out!

Explain to students that humans rely on plants for many things. One of the most important uses of plants is food. Remind students that part of showing good character is respecting nature, which includes plants. For example: hamburgers—buns are made of flour; flour is made from wheat; wheat is a grass (a plant); hamburger meat is beef; beef is made from cows; cows eat grass (a plant); pickles are cucumbers (from a plant), ketchup is made from tomatoes (from a plant).

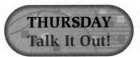
WEDNESDAY
Take It Out!

Bring nature into the classroom. Cover a bulletin board with green butcher paper on the bottom and blue butcher paper on the top. Add a large yellow sun. Provide students with craft materials to make pictures of their favorite parts of nature, such as trees, flowers, the sun, and clouds. Post students' pictures on the display.

Take-Home Activity: Have students ask their parents what they think is the most important part of nature and why.

THURSDAY
Talk It Out!

Have group time outside and sit in the grass. Allow students to share parents' responses about the most important parts of nature.

FRIDAY
Act It Out!

Help students appreciate nature by performing the following movements. Encourage students to act them out in slow motion.
1. an autumn leaf from a tree and tumbling to the ground
2. a growing seed moistened by rain that sprouts, grows, and blooms
3. a tuft of grass enduring the rain and wind of a thunderstorm
4. an ocean wave starts as a swell, becomes a large wave, and crashes on the shore

End the activity by singing "If You Have Character and You Know It."

Be a Good Citizen by Respecting Wildlife

Objective: Students will learn that being a good citizen means respecting all creatures.

MONDAY
Check It Out!

Read aloud the following quote.

In the days of perfect nature, man lived together with birds and beasts, and there was no distinction of their kind . . . they were in a state of natural integrity. — Chuang-tzu

Discussion Questions:
1. What would our world be like if everyone treated all "birds and beasts" nicely?
2. What are some ways that people and animals are similar?
3. What are some ways that animals show their intelligence?
4. Which animals near your home should you leave alone? Which animals can you help?
5. What can you do to show kindness to animals near your home, such as birds?

TUESDAY
Try It Out!

Explain to students that animals can do amazing things. For example, some birds fly very long distances, such as the arctic tern. It nests close to the north pole in the summer, and in autumn it flies south to Antarctica. Each spring it returns north again. Use a map to show students how long the trip is. Provide students with books about specific animals that can be found in your area. Give students time to read their books, then have each student share an interesting fact that she learned about her animal.

WEDNESDAY
Take It Out!

Have students draw pictures of animals that live near their homes. Provide students with pictures of local animals for inspiration.

Take-Home Activity: Have students share their animal pictures with their parents and label the animals' main parts (such as head, eyes, body, wings, legs, feet, tail, etc.).

THURSDAY
Talk It Out!

During group time, have students share their labeled animal pictures, then post them. Discuss how each animal helps humans and what humans can do to show these animals respect.

FRIDAY
Act It Out!

Give students a way to act on their kindness to wildlife by feeding the birds outside your classroom. Provide each student with "Bird Feeder Craft Directions" (see page 11) and the materials (for each student or pair of students) to make a feeder. If possible, when the feeders are complete, create a permanent bird feeding area so that students can watch the birds.

End the activity by singing "If You Have Character and You Know It."

Be a Good Citizen by Appreciating Nature

Bird Feeders

Peanut Butter and Pretzel Hangers

1. Smear unsalted peanut butter on thick, unsalted pretzels.
2. Dip the pretzel into birdseed to coat the peanut butter.
3. Tie a loop of yarn at the top and hang the feeder from a branch.

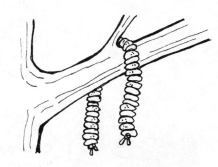

Cereal Feeder

1. Cut a two-foot (60.96 cm) long piece of yarn.
2. Tie a pencil or similarly sized object onto one end of the yarn.
3. String ring-shaped cereal onto the yarn until it is almost full of cereal.
4. Remove the pencil and tie off each end of the yarn.
5. Loop the yarn over a branch.

Apple Treat Feeder

1. Wrap an apple with yarn from top to bottom and tie with a double knot at the top.
2. Repeat two more times at different angles.
3. Create a hanger for the apple by looping yarn through the knots at the top of the apple and hang the feeder from a branch.

Pine Cone Feeder

1. Tie a string around the wide end of a pine cone and secure with a double knot.
2. Make a loop with the string for a hanger.
3. Cover the pine cone with unsalted peanut butter.
4. Roll in birdseed and poke sunflower seeds into the crevices.
5. Hang the feeder from a branch.

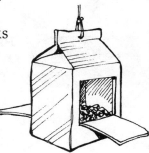

Milk Carton Feeder

1. Cut two-sided windows in opposite sides of a wax carton, leaving a two-inch (5 cm) deep tray at the bottom.
2. Fold the windows down so the bird will have a place to stand as it sticks its head inside the window to get the seeds.
3. Poke one small hole through the top of the carton.
4. Thread heavy string or yarn through the hole to create a loop hanger for the feeder.
5. Fill the bottom of the carton with birdseed or sunflower seeds.
6. Hang the feeder from a branch.

Objective: Students will learn that being a good citizen means knowing about your country.

MONDAY
Check It Out!

Read aloud the book *We the Kids: The Preamble to the Constitution of the United States* by David Catrow (Dial Books for Young Readers, 2002). Three students and a dog learn to find a "more perfect union" while on a camping trip.

Discussion Questions:
1. What do the characters learn in this story?
2. What does it mean to be "united"?
3. Why is it important for the people in your country to respect each other's differences?
4. Why is it important to know about your country and what it stands for?
5. What are some things that you can do to learn about your country?

TUESDAY
Try It Out!

Explain to students that hundreds of years ago, when the United States was a new country, a group of leaders got together to plan how best to organize it. Explain how important documents were written and signed to establish the basis for the country's laws. On a large piece of chart paper, have students make a class "Declaration of Good Citizens." Brainstorm with students things that they can do to make the class, the community, and their country a better place. Post the declaration as a reminder for students that good citizenship starts now.

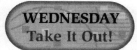
WEDNESDAY
Take It Out!

Provide each student with a copy of the "I Can Be a Good Citizen" worksheet. (See page 13.) Have students brainstorm what it means to be a good citizen. Then, let students fill in their definitions of what good citizenship means on their worksheets.

Take-Home Activity: Allow students to take home their "I Can Be a Good Citizen" worksheets. Have them complete their worksheets with their parents.

THURSDAY
Talk It Out!

During group time, have students share their completed "I Can Be a Good Citizen" worksheets, then post them. List the everyday examples of how to be a good citizen on a piece of poster board titled "My Country Counts Every Day." Display the list in the classroom.

FRIDAY
Act It Out!

Have students work in pairs to role-play examples of good citizenship.

End the activity by singing "If You Have Character and You Know It."

 Daily Character Education • CD-0066 • © Carson-Dellosa

I Can Be a Good Citizen

Take a few minutes to think about what it means to be a good citizen. Then, complete the following statements.

Name _____

Being a good citizen means . . .

_____

_____

Every day I can be a good citizen by . . .

1. _____

_____

2. _____

_____

3. _____

_____

On special days, such as national holidays, I can be a good citizen by . . .

1. _____

_____

2. _____

_____

3. _____

_____

Compassion

Week 5 -Week 8

"If You Have Character and You Know It!"

Sung to the tune:

"If You're Happy and You Know It"

■ ■ ■ ■ ■ ■ ■

Verse 2:
Be compassionate and kind—
  yes sir-eee!
Be compassionate and kind—
  yes sir-eee!
If you care and do things right,
You'll sleep better through the night.
Be compassionate and kind—
  yes sir-eee!

Repeated Verse:
If you have character and you know
  it—let it show!
If you have character and you know
  it—let it show!
In everything along your way,
In all you do and say,
If you have character and you know
  it—let it show!

Dear Parents and Guardians,

For the next four weeks, our class will be discussing ways to demonstrate compassion. We will be singing our theme song, including the new verse about compassion. Please sing the song at home with your child.

On Wednesdays, look for your child to bring home a question or activity to be completed with your help. The assignments are listed below.

Week One: Your child will ask you to share an example of a recent time when someone showed you kindness.

Week Two: Your child will challenge you to complete a word puzzle and turn H-A-T-E into L-O-V-E.

Week Three: Your child will complete a good deed for a member of your family.

Week Four: Your child will tell you about a charity activity that we are completing in our class. He or she might also ask for your advice and assistance to complete the task.

Compassion

Show Compassion by Being Kind

Objective: Students will learn that all deeds of kindness are of value.

MONDAY
Check It Out!

Read aloud the fable "The Lion and the Mouse."

Once upon a time, in a jungle far away, a mouse accidentally ran across the paws of a sleeping lion. The lion woke and roared, "Who stepped on me?" Then, he grabbed the little mouse between two great paws.

"Please, mighty king of the jungle," squeaked the mouse, "Please don't eat me. I am so small. I would hardly be a mouthful. And if you spare me, someday I will return the kindness." The lion laughed at the tiny creature's kind promise and was so amused by the little mouse that he opened his paws and let the mouse go.

Years later, when the lion was roaming in the forest for food, he got entangled in a hunter's net. He struggled with all his might, but the lion couldn't free himself. He opened his mouth and let out a giant roar. The mouse heard the lion's rage echoing through the forest and hurried to help. After assessing the problem, the mouse began gnawing until the ropes fell off and the lion was freed. "Remember," squeaked the mouse at the lion, "No act of kindness, no matter how small, is ever wasted." —Aesop

Discussion Questions:
1. Why did the lion doubt that the mouse would be able to return the favor?
2. Have you ever helped someone who was bigger or older than you?
3. Has someone smaller or younger than you ever helped you?
4. Why do people sometimes think that small or young people cannot help?
5. As a young person, what kinds of things can you do to help others?

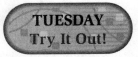

TUESDAY
Try It Out!

Have each student share an example from a book or a movie in which the main character showed kindness to someone. List the examples on the board. Remind students that they can be good examples of kindness.

WEDNESDAY
Take It Out!

Have each student share a time when he showed kindness to someone or when someone showed kindness to him.

Take-Home Activity: Have students ask their parents to share examples of someone showing kindness.

THURSDAY
Talk It Out!

During group time, have students share their parents' stories about kindness.

FRIDAY
Act It Out!

Divide the class into pairs. Each pair should reenact Aesop's fable "The Lion and the Mouse" using two different animals, such as an opossum and bear or a bird and an elephant.

End the activity by singing "If You Have Character and You Know It."

Compassion

Show Compassion by Being Loving

Objective: Students will learn that showing love with words and actions builds compassion.

MONDAY
Check It Out!

Introduce this week's topic by asking students questions about their loved ones.

Discussion Questions:
1. Who are the people you love most?
2. How do you demonstrate your love for them?
3. Why do you think demonstrating love to others is important?
4. How does it make you feel when someone demonstrates love for you?
5. What is your favorite way to say "I love you" with actions instead of words?

TUESDAY
Try It Out!

Ask each student to make a list of people he loves, including family members and friends. Next to each person's name, have him write what makes each of them lovable. Encourage willing students to read their lists of loved ones and explain what they love about each of them. On the board, keep tallies of characteristics that make people lovable. As a class, note the characteristics that make people most lovable. For follow-up, have each student choose someone on his list and write him an "I Love You Letter." Students should name several things that the person does that makes him easy to love. Have students deliver or mail their letters.

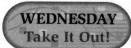
WEDNESDAY
Take It Out!

Ask students if it is possible to turn hate into love. Then, give them the following word puzzle to solve. Write the letters H-A-T-E on the board. Then, tell students that they can change one letter with each word move, but it must spell a new word. (Provide dictionaries if needed.) Challenge students to turn H-A-T-E into L-O-V-E with various numbers of word moves.
Answers may vary: four moves—hate, have, cave, cove, love; four moves—hate, have, rave, rove, love; five moves—hate, have, hive, dive, dove, love

Take-Home Activity: Have students challenge their parents with the word puzzle. Ask students to record the solutions.

THURSDAY
Talk It Out!

During group time, have students share solutions to the puzzle. Then, make a list on the board of ways to actually change hate into love (for example, genuinely listen to others, ask forgiveness, demonstrate caring through actions).

FRIDAY
Act It Out!

Divide the class into groups of three. Have the groups role-play various situations in which one member is sad and explains why. The other two should cheer the sad student with encouraging words.
Examples of sad situations:
1. moving far away
2. losing a pet
3. losing something valuable

End the activity by singing "If You Have Character and You Know It."

Compassion

Show Compassion by Being Helpful

Objective: Students will learn that being helpful shows compassion.

MONDAY
Check It Out!

Read aloud the book *Doctor De Soto* by William Steig (Sunburst, 1990). A mouse dentist is helpful—even to a fox who wants to eat him.

Discussion Questions:
1. Why was the mouse helpful to the fox?
2. How have you helped someone recently?
3. How does it feel to know that you have helped someone?
4. As a class, what can we do each day to be helpful to each other?
5. What can you do to help at home?

TUESDAY
Try It Out!

Recognize and celebrate students' good deeds with a bulletin board entitled "We Fall for Helping Hands." Cover the top third of the bulletin board with blue butcher paper and add cotton-ball clouds. Using paper grocery bags, cut out the shape of tree trunk and attach it to the center bottom of the bulletin board. Copy a "Helping Hands" pattern for each student. (See page 18.) Using colored pencils, have each student color his pattern with fall leaf colors. Encourage each student to tell about the good deeds he has recently performed. On their hand shapes, have students write about their helping experiences. Attach the "helping hands" to the tree. Add hand leaves as you see or hear students doing helpful deeds.

WEDNESDAY
Take It Out!

Ask each student to select a family member at home who would appreciate his help today.

Take-Home Activity: Challenge each student to do a good deed today for the family member who could use her help (for example, take out the garbage for her brother or help her mom fold clothes).

THURSDAY
Talk It Out!

During group time, have students share their good deeds. Have them tell about the reactions from the people helped, as well as how they felt doing the helpful acts.

FRIDAY
Act It Out!

Have volunteers act out scenes from the book *Doctor De Soto*. Allow students to discuss what they would have done if they were in Doctor De Soto's situation. Take a poll to see which students would have helped the fox.

End the activity by singing "If You Have Character and You Know It."

Helping Hands
Patterns

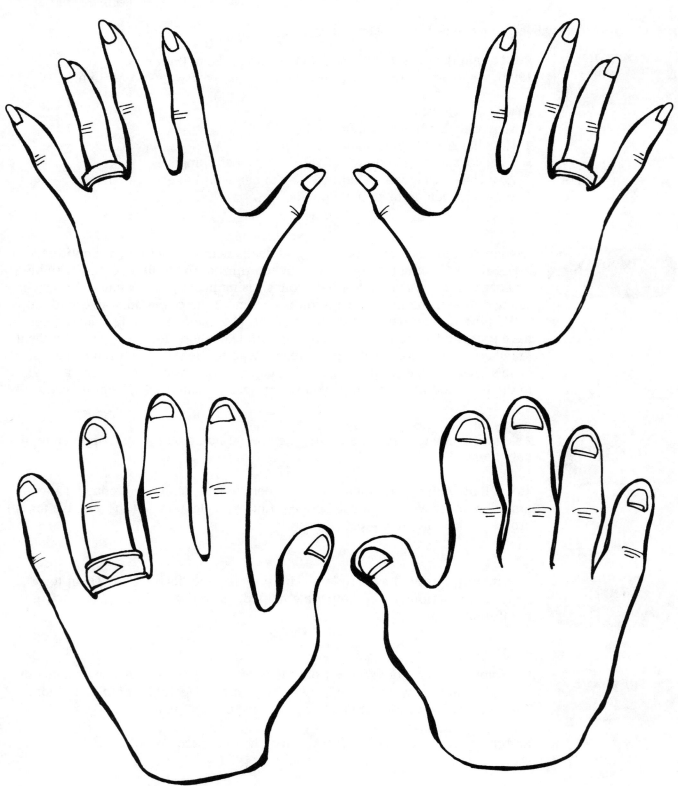

Compassion

Show Compassion through Giving

Objective: Students will learn they can be compassionate by providing charity to those in need.

MONDAY
Check It Out!

Read aloud the book *The Rag Coat* by Lauren A. Mills (Little, Brown & Co., 1991). A girl has a patchwork coat full of stories.

Discussion Questions:
1. Why is the girl so proud of her coat made of scraps?
2. Have you ever heard someone make fun of a less fortunate person?
3. How should those in need be treated?
4. Why do you think some people are charitable and others are not?
5. What can you give to those in need?

TUESDAY
Try It Out!

Ask students to think about times when they needed something. Perhaps they needed a telephone to call for a ride, or they needed someone to help them study for a test. Have students brainstorm the kinds of feelings associated with being in need, such as desperation, sadness, fright, etc. Remind students to be sensitive to the feelings of others when they see someone in need.

WEDNESDAY
Take It Out!

Challenge each students to think of a charitable deed that she can perform this week. Brainstorm ideas on the board.
Project Examples:
1. Donate previously read storybooks to the local library.
2. Gather good, old toys and give them to a local shelter.
3. Ask permission from parents to visit an elderly family member.
4. Make a get-well card and mail it to someone you know who is sick.

Take-Home Activity: Have students explain to their parents the charitable deeds they would like to perform, and ask for their advice and assistance.

THURSDAY
Talk It Out!

During group time, have students share the charitable deeds that they have selected and when they will perform them. Tell students that they will need to make specific plans to complete their charitable deeds.

FRIDAY
Act It Out!

Give students time in class to plan out and write down the steps needed to complete their charitable deeds. Have each student share her plan with a classmate.

End the activity by singing "If You Have Character and You Know It."

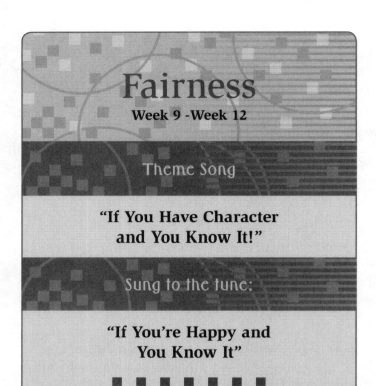

Fairness

Week 9 -Week 12

Theme Song

"If You Have Character and You Know It!"

Sung to the tune:

"If You're Happy and You Know It"

■ ■ ■ ■ ■ ■ ■

Verse 3:
Be fair with a peaceful heart—
    yes sir-eee!
Be fair with a peaceful heart—
    yes sir-eee!
If you play by every rule,
Working with others can be cool.
Be fair with a peaceful heart—
    yes sir-eee!

Repeated Verse:
If you have character and you know
    it—let it show!
If you have character and you know
    it—let it show!
In everything along your way,
In all you do and say,
If you have character and you know
    it—let it show!

Dear Parents and Guardians,

For the next four weeks, our class will be working on ways to demonstrate fairness. We will be singing our theme song, including the new verse about a peaceful heart. Please sing the song at home with your child.

On Wednesdays, look for your child to bring home a question or activity to be completed with your help. The assignments are listed below.

Week One: Your child will explain to you the four steps for working out conflicts. Then, together you will complete the "S.T.O.P. Conflict" worksheet.

Week Two: Your child will list all of the ways he or she is like and different from his or her best friend. After sharing the list with you, your child will explain what we are learning in class about appreciating the similarities and differences among people.

Week Three: Your child will ask you what you think can be done to stop bullying at school. Then, you and your child can make a list of ways to encourage students to treat others fairly.

Week Four: Your child will ask you why you think it is important for people to follow the rules.

Fairness

Be Fair by Solving Disagreements Peacefully

Objective: Students will learn the value of solving disagreements fairly.

**MONDAY
Check It Out!**

Read aloud the book *Why Are You Fighting, Davy?* by Brigitte Weninger (North South Books, 1999). Two rabbits learn a lesson about getting along.

Discussion Questions:
1. What were the two friends disagreeing about?
2. When you disagree with a friend, should you just give in and do what he says?
3. When you disagree with a friend, should you always get your way?
4. Can most disagreements between friends be solved?
5. When two friends disagree, how can they settle the problem so that they will both feel good about it?

**TUESDAY
Try It Out!**

On the board, list the four steps to peacefully S.T.O.P. a conflict. Go over these with students.
1. **S**top—don't let the conflict get worse. It will make solving the problem easier.
2. **T**alk—discuss the conflict. What is causing the disagreement?
3. **O**ffer—brainstorm and share some positive options. How could both your needs be meet and still be fair?
4. **P**ick—select one of the positive options that each of you agree upon. If you still can't agree, ask a trusted friend or adult to help resolve the conflict.

**WEDNESDAY
Take It Out!**

Give each student a copy of the "S.T.O.P. Conflict" worksheet. (See page 22.) Brainstorm sentences that students can write for each step of stopping conflict. Then, have students complete the top portion in class.

Take-Home Activity: Have students explain to their parents the four steps to peacefully resolving a conflict. Together, have them complete the rest of the "S.T.O.P. Conflict" worksheets.

**THURSDAY
Talk It Out!**

During group time, have students share their pictures showing how to end conflict from the "S.T.O.P. Conflict" worksheet.

**FRIDAY
Act It Out!**

Divide the class into groups of three. Give each group a conflict situation to role-play. Have two students enact the situation, then have the third student explain ways to resolve the problem.
Sample situations:
1. Two siblings want to watch television. One has a homework assignment to watch the evening news. The other wants to watch his favorite program.
2. Two friends want to ride the swings. There is only one swing open.
3. Two classmates have stayed after school to finish their science projects. There is only one piece of poster board left, and they both want to use it.

End the activity by singing "If You Have Character and You Know It."

Be Fair by Solving Disagreements Peacefully

S.T.O.P. Conflict

Write a sentence using fair words to say during each stage of stopping conflict. In the boxes, draw pictures showing the S.T.O.P. stages.

Name _____

What to say to S.T.O.P. conflict . . .

Stop: _____

Talk: _____

Offer: _____

Pick: _____

Draw a picture that shows what you might do at each step.

STOP	TALK

OFFER	PICK

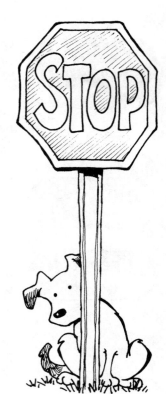

Daily Character Education • CD-0066 • © Carson-Dellosa

Fairness

Be Fair by Appreciating Differences

Objective: Students will learn to show fairness by learning from each other's differences.

MONDAY
Check It Out!

Read aloud the book *Mr. Lincoln's Way* by Patricia Polacco (Philomel, 2001). A boy learns that the differences in people should be valued.

Discussion Questions:
1. How does the principal show the bully that differences in people are okay?
2. Why do some people fear things or people that are strange or new to them?
3. Is it fair to treat someone badly who looks different from you?
4. Have you seen someone treated unfairly because of how she looks?
5. Can you learn from people who look different from you?

TUESDAY
Try It Out!

Begin this lesson by playing a game. Conduct different rounds by having students group themselves according to each of these categories: hair color, eye color, gender, birthday months, birthplace (all those born in the same state or city), clothes (certain colors or styles), favorite colors. Each time after the groups are sorted, give each member of the smallest group a small treat or verbal praise. After the game, discuss how students felt when they were in a group that didn't receive anything. Explain that not being fair to others based on outward characteristics is unfair. End by giving each student a small treat or verbal praise for cooperating.

WEDNESDAY
Take It Out!

Invite students to think about their best friends. On a piece of paper, have each student list all of the ways she is like her best friend.

Take-Home Activity: Have students finish their best friend lists by using the backs of their papers to list all of the ways they are different from their best friends. Encourage students to share their lists with their parents to show that they are learning about appreciating the differences, as well as the similarities, that people have.

THURSDAY
Talk It Out!

During group time, have students share their best friend lists. Remind students that each person is unique and that our differences allow us to learn from each other.

FRIDAY
Act It Out!

Present students with the following situation: you wake up in the morning and your skin is green and you have an extra arm. Ask students how they might be treated differently by others. After students respond, remind them that although people cannot control many of their physical characteristics (skin color, gender, height, etc.), they can control their actions and attitudes about others.

End the activity by singing "If You Have Character and You Know It."

Fairness

Be Fair by Not Bullying

Objective: Students will learn that bullying behavior is not an acceptable or fair way to treat people.

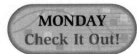

MONDAY
Check It Out!

Read aloud the book *The Recess Queen* by Alexis O'Neill (Scholastic, 2002). The new girl befriends Milly Jean, the recess queen.

Discussion Questions:
1. How is the school bully changed in the story?
2. What does it mean to be a bully?
3. How does bullying behavior make other people feel?
4. Why is it wrong to participate in any sort of bullying situation (either being the bully or encouraging the behavior)?
5. What can you do to calm a bullying situation?

TUESDAY
Try It Out!

Have students share examples of bullying situations they have witnessed or experienced. After students respond, ask them why they think bullies act a certain way. Share with students that bullying behavior is usually a result of the person feeling bad about herself. A bully often tries to make others feel worse than she feels about herself. Also, explain that victims of bullies do not deserve the bullying treatment and should try to find ways to make the unfair treatment end.

WEDNESDAY
Take It Out!

Ask students to share their ideas about how to handle bullying behavior. As a class, discuss each suggestion to determine its effectiveness and appropriateness.

Take-Home Activity: Have students ask their parents what they think can be done to stop bullying at school. Then, have each student work with his parents to make a list of ways to encourage people to treat each other fairly.

THURSDAY
Talk It Out!

During group time, have students share the lists the parents and students wrote together. Incorporate the best ideas by listing them on poster board to display as positive reminders.

FRIDAY
Act It Out!

Conduct class role plays, pretending that you are the bully. Provide bullying situations for students to role-play appropriate reactions with you.
Sample situations:
1. older bully making fun of a younger student at the bus stop
2. a bully chasing away a student who wants to play on the playground swings
3. a bully threatening a classmate to give him the answers for homework
4. a bully making fun of a student for what she is wearing

End the activity by singing "If You Have Character and You Know It."

Objective: Students will learn that being fair means accepting and following rules.

**MONDAY
Check It Out!**

Read aloud the fable "The Donkey and the Lion."

Once upon a time, a donkey and a lion agreed to join together so that they could capture more prey. The lion had great strength; the donkey had great speed. After capturing as much prey as they could in one day, the lion divided the catch into three equal stacks. "I will take the first share," roared the lion, "because I am king of the jungle. I will take the second share for I was a partner in the chase. And the third share, I will also take, because if you take it, I think it will be a source of great evil to you—it might even cost you your life." The lion smiled. Although it was unfair, the donkey understood the lion's new rules of food division and set off as fast as his legs would carry him. —Aesop

Discussion Questions:
1. How did the lion get away with taking all of the food?
2. Have you ever played with someone who made up their own rules?
3. How does it feel to be cheated or taken advantage of?
4. Why is it important to play by rules that all players agree upon?
5. When playing a game or participating in a group activity, what can you do to make sure that everyone is treated fairly?

**TUESDAY
Try It Out!**

Complete this experiment with students. Give a few students blue stickers to attach to their shirts. Then, give all other students yellow stickers to attach to their shirts. Tell students that everyone who wears a yellow sticker will get to go to recess five minutes early. At dismissal time, excuse students wearing blue stickers early. When students object, tell them you decided to change the rules and didn't think to tell them. Then, point out how what you did was unfair. Discuss why it is important and fair for everyone to know and follow the rules.

**WEDNESDAY
Take It Out!**

Invite each student to share an experience when someone didn't follow the rules.

Take-Home Activity: Have students ask their parents why they feel it is important for people to follow the rules.

**THURSDAY
Talk It Out!**

During group time, have students share what their parents said about following rules. On chart paper, make a list of good reasons to follow rules titled "Fairness Rules!"

**FRIDAY
Act It Out!**

Invite three student volunteers to role-play the following situation: During dodgeball games, one student often throws the ball at players' heads (which is against the rules). Another student asks to sit out during dodgeball, because he has been hit in the head several times. The third student is a fair and good player, but she is bothered that her friend doesn't want to play. After the students act out the situation, have students from the audience comment about how each dodgeball player feels and suggest ways to resolve the unfair situation.

End the activity by singing "If You Have Character and You Know It."

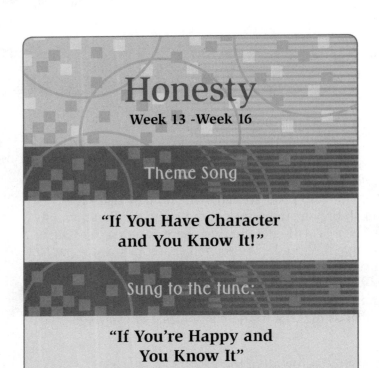

Honesty

Week 13 - Week 16

Theme Song

"If You Have Character and You Know It!"

Sung to the tune:

"If You're Happy and You Know It"

■ ■ ■ ■ ■ ■ ■

Verse 4:
Be honest; tell the truth—yes sir-eee!
Be honest; tell the truth—yes sir-eee!
If you don't steal, cheat, or lie,
You won't need an alibi.
Be honest; tell the truth—yes sir-eee!

Repeated Verse:
If you have character and you know
    it—let it show!
If you have character and you know
    it—let it show!
In everything along your way,
In all you do and say,
If you have character and you know
    it—let it show!

Dear Parents and Guardians,

For the next four weeks, our class will be exploring ways to demonstrate honesty. We will be singing our theme song, including the new verse about truth. Please sing the song at home with your child.

On Wednesdays, look for your child to bring home a question or activity to be completed with your help. The assignments are listed below.

Week One: Your child will ask you to share something about yourself that you are proud of.

Week Two: Your child will ask you to help him or her complete the "May I Take It" worksheet.

Week Three: Your child will talk with you about why it is important to have a reputation for being honest.

Week Four: Your child will ask you how long you think it takes to regain someone's trust after telling a lie.

Honesty

Be Honest by Being True to Yourself

Objective: Students will learn that being honest means being true to yourself and proud of who you are.

MONDAY Check It Out!

Read aloud the fable "The Donkey in Lion's Clothes."

Once upon a time, a donkey found the skin of a lion. The donkey wore the lion's skin like a coat. He pretended to be a lion and frightened the animals by strutting around. Of course he didn't roar, because donkeys do not roar well.

All went well for the pretend lion until one day he ran into a fox. At first the fox was frightened by the donkey in lion's clothes. Seeing the fox's fear, the donkey puffed up and tried to roar like a lion. As soon as the fox heard the familiar bray of a donkey, he laughed and said, "I might have been afraid of you, if you had kept your mouth shut. But now I see that you are nothing but a big lie." —Aesop

Discussion Questions:
1. What was the lesson in the story of "The Donkey in the Lion's Clothes"?
2. Have you ever pretended to be something you are not to impress someone?
3. Do you sometimes wish that you had something or could do something to make yourself stand out?
4. What about you makes you proud of yourself?
5. Why do you think it is important to be comfortable with who you are?

TUESDAY Try It Out!

Provide students with craft materials and drawing paper to illustrate pictures of themselves. Encourage students to emphasize the features and talents they possess that make them proud. Display the pictures on a bulletin board titled "Proud of Who We Are!"

WEDNESDAY Take It Out!

Have students brainstorm a list of things that all students in the class can be proud of (for example, over half the class was on the honor roll, perfect attendance last week, etc.). Point out that because they have such wonderful characteristics, they should be proud of who they are and not waste time pretending to be somebody else.

Take-Home Activity: Have students ask their parents about something about themselves that they are proud of.

THURSDAY Talk It Out!

During group time, have students share some things that their parents are proud of. Discuss the similarities and differences between the students' and adult's answers.

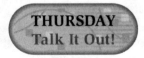 **FRIDAY Act It Out!**

Remind students about Monday's fable about the donkey. Have students take turns sharing advice that they would offer the donkey so that he might feel better about who he is and not feel he must pretend to be something he is not.

End the activity by singing "If You Have Character and You Know It."

Honesty

Be Honest by Not Stealing

Objective: Students will learn it is dishonest to steal from others.

MONDAY
Check It Out!

Read aloud the book *The Real Thief* by William Steig (Farrar, Straus and Giroux, 1985). A loyal goose is falsely accused of stealing.

Discussion Questions:
1. How do they realize that the goose is not the thief?
2. Why should you not steal from others?
3. What must store owners do when items get stolen?
4. Who gets hurt when someone steals?
5. Why is it important to respect the property of others?

TUESDAY
Try It Out!

Discuss with students that it is important to understand the full meaning of stealing. Give students several examples and have students vote on and discuss which situations are examples of stealing.

Sample situations:
1. taking money from a parent's purse or wallet without asking permission
2. eating candy that belongs to a sibling
3. taking a dollar found on the ground at a public place
4. finding and keeping a seashell from the beach
5. keeping extra change accidentally given by a store clerk

WEDNESDAY
Take It Out!

Provide each student with a copy of "May I Take It?" (See page 29.) Explain the directions and do the first example together.

Take-Home Activity: Have students complete the "May I Take It?" worksheet with their parents.

THURSDAY
Talk It Out!

During group time, have students share their responses from the "May I Take It?" worksheets. Remind students that even though not all of the situations were examples of stealing, if in doubt, they should leave the "found" object alone.

FRIDAY
Act It Out!

Have three students volunteer to role-play the following situation: Three close friends go into a toy store at the mall. One friend says that he is planning on taking a toy without paying for it. The other two friends have never shoplifted before, but they both feel like it would not be right to watch their friend take the toy. After watching the role play, have the student audience offer suggestions of how the two friends should appropriately respond.

End the activity by singing "If You Have Character and You Know It."

 Daily Character Education • CD-0066 • © Carson-Dellosa

Be Honest by Not Stealing

May I Take It?

Read each situation. Place an X beside each example of stealing, a question mark beside each that is not an example of stealing but good judgement should be used before taking, and a check mark if it is okay to take.

Name _____

_____ a coin found on the floor of the school bus

_____ a pretty leaf on the ground in your grandparents' backyard

_____ a wallet found in a parking lot in front of a store

_____ a half-eaten candy bar that your brother left on the kitchen table

_____ a stone found on a lake shore

_____ a piece of cake from an uncut, decorated cake on the counter

_____ a sweater found on the playground after school

_____ a smashed, but clean, cupcake your friend is planning to throw away

_____ a golf ball you find in the lake at the golf course

_____ an egg from a bird's nest found at your school playground

_____ an apple from the tree in your backyard

_____ a few grapes from a fruit stand in the grocery store

_____ a marble from a friend's marble collection when he's not looking

_____ a coin that you found on the sidewalk

_____ a dollar from your mom's purse for your lunch money

_____ a coin found in the coin return slot in a telephone booth

_____ your sister's pencil from her backpack

_____ a stamp you found in your dad's desk that he plans to use to mail a letter to your grandmother

_____ an extra dollar in change that a fast food cashier accidentally gives you

_____ a ten-dollar bill your aunt offers as a gift

_____ an orange from a neighbor's tree

_____ a stick you found at a national park

_____ a library book found on a bus stop bench

_____ a flower blooming in a neighbor's yard

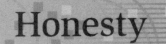
Honesty

Be Honest by Not Cheating

Objective: Students will understand what cheating is and how it can harm your character.

MONDAY
Check It Out!

Read aloud the book *Junie B., First Grader: Cheater Pants* by Barbara Park (Random House, 2003). A student learns a valuable lesson about cheating.

Discussion Questions:
1. When does the girl learn her lesson about cheating?
2. What does it mean to cheat?
3. Is it cheating if you copy your friend's homework paper?
4. Is it cheating if you get help with a class assignment from your parent?
5. Why is it important not to cheat?

TUESDAY
Try It Out!

On the board, make a list of who each student says is her hero. When the list is complete, ask students, "Is anyone on this list known for being a cheater?" Explain that those held in high esteem are usually those with good character. Find out how many students would like to be a person that others look up to. Discuss ways they can be that kind of person. Then, have each student draw a self-portrait. Display the portraits on a bulletin board titled "Tomorrow's Heroes."

WEDNESDAY
Take It Out!

As a class, discuss why it is important to be someone that people trust and look up to. Ask students for suggestions about how to get and maintain positive reputations.

Take-Home Activity: Have students talk to their parents about why it is important to have a reputation for being honest.

THURSDAY
Talk It Out!

During group time, have students share the discussions they had with their parents about having a reputation for honesty.

FRIDAY
Act It Out!

Divide the class into pairs. Each pair should role-play what to say in situations in order to maintain a good name and reputation.
Sample situations:
1. a classmate asks to copy your homework
2. a friend urges you to let him look at your paper during a test
3. your mom accidentally gives you extra money for allowance
4. your brother divides a bag of candy and unknowingly gives you extra pieces

End the activity by singing "If You Have Character and You Know It."

Objective: Students will learn that lying destroys trust.

**MONDAY
Check It Out!**

Read aloud the fable "The Wolf and the Sheep"

Once upon a time, a wolf lay sick in his lair. In need of nourishment, he beckoned a passing sheep, "If you will fetch me some water from the stream, then I will be strong enough to go out and get myself some food."

The smart sheep, recognizing a lie when he heard it said, "Yes, I am sure of that. If I bring you water, you will no doubt have the strength to make me your dinner." —Aesop

Discussion Questions:
1. How does the sheep know that he would be the wolf's food?
2. Why do people tell lies?
3. When you know that someone tells lies, what do you think about her?
4. How do you feel after telling a lie?
5. Why is it important to not tell lies?

**TUESDAY
Try It Out!**

Allow students to demonstrate their understanding of honesty. Cover a horizontal bulletin board in green paper. Add simple designs in the corners to look like a dollar bill. Have each student write a brief fable about a character who is honest that results in a happy ending. Post the stories on the bulletin board. Title the display "It Pays to Be Honest."

**WEDNESDAY
Take It Out!**

Have students read aloud the fables they wrote yesterday.

Take-Home Activity: Have students ask their parents how long they think it takes to regain someone's trust after telling a lie.

**THURSDAY
Talk It Out!**

During group time, have students share the results of their parents' responses. Encourage students to share examples of times when they have lied to their parents. Then, ask them to discuss situations in which they have been lied to. See if students can agree with how long it takes to regain someone's trust after a person tells a lie.

**FRIDAY
Act It Out!**

Allow students work in small groups to act out some of the fables they wrote on Tuesday.

End the activity by singing "If You Have Character and You Know It."

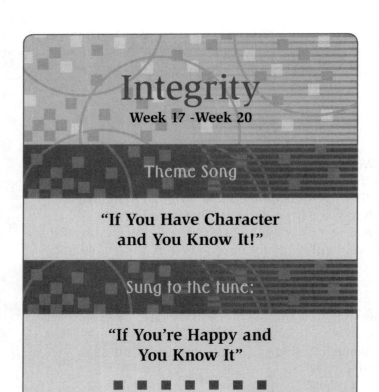

Integrity

Week 17 - Week 20

Theme Song

"If You Have Character and You Know It!"

Sung to the tune:

"If You're Happy and You Know It"

■ ■ ■ ■ ■ ■ ■

Verse 5:
Have integrity; do your best—
    yes sir-eee!
Have integrity; do your best—
    yes sir-eee!
And deep down in your heart,
You will always do your part.
Have integrity; do your best—
    yes sir-eee!

Repeated Verse:
If you have character and you know
    it—let it show!
If you have character and you know
    it—let it show!
In everything along your way,
In all you do and say,
If you have character and you know
    it—let it show!

Dear Parents and Guardians,

For the next four weeks, our class will be discussing ways to demonstrate integrity. We will be singing our theme song, including the new verse about doing your best. Please sing the song at home with your child.

On Wednesdays, look for your child to bring home a question or activity to be completed with your help. The assignments are listed below.

Week One: Your child will ask for your advice on what to do when someone is challenging his or her beliefs or opinions.

Week Two: Your child will ask you to make up a rule to help others better appreciate themselves. For example, comparing yourself to others is a bad habit. Decide to concentrate on yourself, not others.

Week Three: Your child will share a goal that he or she has set. Please share your best advice about how to accomplish the goal.

Week Four: Your child will ask for your advice about how to work in a small group to achieve a goal.

Daily Character Education • CD-0066 • © Carson-Dellosa

Integrity

Have Integrity by Thinking for Yourself

Objective: Students will learn to stand up for what they think.

**MONDAY
Check It Out!**

Read or tell Hans Christian Anderson's story, "The Emperor's New Clothes."

Discussion Questions:
1. Why were the emperor and his people not willing to admit that they could not see the new clothes?
2. Why is it sometimes hard to stand up for what you think is right?
3. If you think a particular way about something, but your friends tell you to think something else, should you be true to your original idea or go along with what they say?
4. Who influences your decisions most?
5. What strategies can you use to make sure that you believe what is right, even if others believe something else?

**TUESDAY
Try It Out!**

Remind students about yesterday's story. Ask students how many would have pretended to see the emperor's clothes. Challenge students to rewrite the ending of "The Emperor's New Clothes" from when the emperor is about to parade through town. Read the new endings aloud to the class.

**WEDNESDAY
Take It Out!**

Ask each students to share a time when she had to stand up for something that she believed in. Have students share what they consider to be the hardest parts in doing so.

Take-Home Activity: Have students ask their parents for their advice about what to do when someone is challenging your beliefs or opinions.

**THURSDAY
Talk It Out!**

During group time, have students share the advice their parents gave them about having beliefs or opinions challenged. As a class, make a list of ways for students to stand up for themselves in these types of situations.

**FRIDAY
Act It Out!**

Share the following quote by Aesop: "By endeavoring to please everybody, you will end up pleasing nobody." Have students take turns explaining what this quote means to them. Post the quote in the classroom as a reminder for students to be proud to think for themselves.

End the activity by singing "If You Have Character and You Know It."

Objective: Students will learn the value of appreciating themselves as special individuals.

MONDAY
Check It Out!

Begin this week's topic by explaining to students that the most important thing about people is who they are on the inside, not by the things they own. Explain that if they are happy with who they are, it is a gift that will make them feel richer and more content.

Discussion Questions:
1. What is something that you do very well?
2. What is one thing about yourself that makes you feel especially proud?
3. How do you feel when someone pays you a compliment?
4. Do you ever stop to think about the different skills, talents, and characteristics you have?
5. Do you spend time comparing yourself to what other people have or can do?

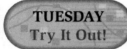
TUESDAY
Try It Out!

Have students write acrostic poems about themselves that celebrate their own unique characteristics and talents. Each student may use single words, phrases, or sentences for each letter in his name. Post the poems around the classroom.

For example:
Jokes around a lot
Easy to make laugh
Reads quickly
Excellent video game player
Might be a police officer someday
You might like him

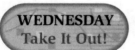
WEDNESDAY
Take It Out!

Have students brainstorm a list of rules to follow to better appreciate themselves. Write the rules on a piece of chart paper.

For example:
1. Avoid comparing yourself to others.
2. Think about all of the things that you do well.
3. When you don't achieve something, remember times when you have succeeded.
4. Be proud of your successes.

Take-Home Activity: Have each student ask her parents to make up a rule to help others better appreciate themselves.

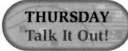
THURSDAY
Talk It Out!

During group time, have students share the additional rules that their parents wrote. Add them to the class list.

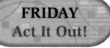
FRIDAY
Act It Out!

Have each student share at least one thing that he appreciates about a classmate until each student has been acknowledged.

End the activity by singing "If You Have Character and You Know It."

34

Integrity

Have Integrity by Doing Your Very Best

Objective: Students will learn that doing their best will help them reach their goals.

MONDAY
Check It Out!

Read aloud the book *Wombat Divine* by Mem Fox (Voyager, 1999). A wombat keeps trying and finally finds the perfect part for himself in a play.

Discussion Questions:
1. Does the Wombat's persistence pay off?
2. Have you ever had to keep trying something before you could do it?
3. How does it feel when you try really hard at something and are able to do it?
4. What does it mean to try your best?
5. Does being the best that you can be mean being perfect?

TUESDAY
Try It Out!

Challenge students to choose something they do that they would like to do better or something that they would like to learn to do. Have them draw themselves accomplishing their goals. Collect the pictures for tomorrow's follow-up activity.

WEDNESDAY
Take It Out!

Return the students' pictures from yesterday's class. On the backs of the pictures, have students write the steps they will take to accomplish their goals. Remind them that "trying my best" should be a step they list.

Take-Home Activity: Have students share the goals that they have set for themselves with their parents. Have students ask them for their best advice about how to accomplish the goals.

THURSDAY
Talk It Out!

During group time, have students share the advice and encouragement their parents offered about accomplishing their goals. Offer students your advice as well, using a personal example of a goal that you accomplished.

FRIDAY
Act It Out!

Pair each student with a classmate so that they can encourage each other toward their goals. Provide students with poster board and markers. Have each student design a "You Can Do It" poster for her partner. Post the students' goal pictures from Tuesday's class beside their encouraging posters.

End the activity by singing "If You Have Character and You Know It."

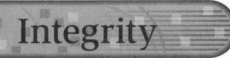

Integrity

Have Integrity by Working Well with Others

Objective: Students will learn that working together in harmony gets things done.

**MONDAY
Check It Out!**

Read aloud the fable "The Father and His Sons."

    Once upon a time, there was a man who had three sons who often argued. The father wanted to show his sons the evils of not working well with others. One day, he brought the sons together and showed them a bundle of sticks. One at a time, he placed the bundle of sticks in each son's hand and told him to break it. Each tried with all his might, but none could do it. Then the father untied the bundle of sticks, and he put one stick into each son's hand. Separately, the sticks broke easily. The man said, "My sons, if you are of one mind—united and willing to help each other—you will be as the bundle of sticks, safe from all attempts of your enemies. If you are divided among yourselves and left alone, you will be broken as easily as the sticks." —Aesop

Discussion Questions:
1. How did the man teach his sons that it was bad to argue all of the time?
2. Do you quarrel with your family members?
3. Do you think it is important for people in groups to get along? Why?
4. Do you ever have trouble working with someone else on a task or project?
5. How does it make you feel when you have trouble working with others?

**TUESDAY
Try It Out!**

Divide the class into four groups. Announce that they will make music. When signaled, one group should clap in unison; one group should whistle a tune; one group should slap the floor rhythmically; and one group should make continuous snapping sounds with their fingers. Explain that each group should make its sound when you point to the group. The object is for each group to get coordinated, and then get all four groups to play as a group. Practice until the individual sounds unite. End by explaining that while it can take time to get people to work together, the harmonious result is worth the effort.

**WEDNESDAY
Take It Out!**

Ask students to share their suggestions of how to best work in small groups to achieve goals.

Take-Home Activity: Have students ask their parents for tips on how to best work in small groups to achieve goals.

**THURSDAY
Talk It Out!**

During group time, have students share their parents' tips about working with others in small groups.

**FRIDAY
Act It Out!**

Divide the class into groups of four. Remind students of the suggestions shared this week about working together. Give each group an assignment to complete that can best be achieved by working in a group, such as cleaning up a center. When students have completed their tasks and returned to their seats, ask them how long it would have taken them to get all of the tasks assigned, organized, and completed if the tasks had been done individually. Point out that working well together can help accomplish some goals faster and more efficiently.

End the activity by singing "If You Have Character and You Know It."

 Daily Character Education • CD-0066 • © Carson-Dellosa

Perseverance

Week 21—Week 23

Theme Song

"If You Have Character and You Know It!"

Sung to the tune:

"If You're Happy and You Know It"

■ ■ ■ ■ ■ ■ ■

Verse 6:
Persevere by sticking to it—
 yes sir-eee!
Persevere by sticking to it—
 yes sir-eee!
If you're patient and you try,
Your only limit is the sky.
Persevere by sticking to it—
 yes sir-eee!

Repeated Verse:
If you have character and you know
 it—let it show!
If you have character and you know
 it—let it show!
In everything along your way,
In all you do and say,
If you have character and you know
 it—let it show!

Dear Parents and Guardians,

For the next three weeks, our class will be working on ways to demonstrate perseverance. We will be singing our theme song, including the new verse about sticking to it. Please sing the song at home with your child.

On Wednesdays, look for your child to bring home a question or activity to be completed with your help. The assignments are listed below.

Week One: Your child will ask you to help him or her complete the "Trying My Patience" worksheet.

Week Two: Your child will ask you to help him or her come up with suggestions for overcoming an obstacle.

Week Three: Your child will ask you to help him or her complete the "Balancing Work and Play" worksheet.

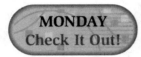  

Perseverance

Persevere by Having Patience

Objective: Students will learn that patience pays off.

MONDAY
Check It Out!

Read aloud the book *Moose, of Course!* by Lynn Plourde (Down East Books, 1999). A young boy learns that sometimes being patient is the best way to get what you want.

Discussion Questions:
1. Does the boy's patience pay off?
2. Why is being patient sometimes difficult?
3. Has there been a situation recently in which you have shown patience?
4. In what types of situations are you least patient?
5. Are there ways to improve your patience in situations when you must wait?

TUESDAY
Try It Out!

Tell students that you will give out candy. They will have three options in how they choose to receive it. They can have a piece immediately; they can wait and have two pieces of candy in an hour; or, if they wait two hours, they will receive five pieces of candy. Allow students to make their individual choices. When the last student has been given the candy (probably at least one will opt for the two-hour wait), discuss how sometimes learning to wait patiently provides a bigger reward.

WEDNESDAY
Take It Out!

Provide each student with the "Trying My Patience" worksheet. (See page 39.) Read the situations on the worksheet to students.

Take-Home Activity: Have students take home their copies of "Trying My Patience" to complete with their parents.

THURSDAY
Talk It Out!

During group time, have students share their responses from "Trying My Patience."

FRIDAY
Act It Out!

Divide the class into pairs and have each pair role-play one of the three situations from the "Trying My Patience" worksheet.

End the activity by singing "If You Have Character and You Know It."

Trying My Patience

Read the following situations. Then, decide which would be the most appropriate, patient response.

Name _____

Situation 1

Your teacher gave a small group assignment to make a poster. There is only one bottle of glue for all groups to use, and the poster must be completed by the end of the school day. In this situation you would . . .

- ask a person in the group who is using the glue when your group can use it
- give up on the project since it might not get done in time if you wait for the glue
- when the group next to you is not looking, take the glue from their work table

Situation 2

A friend borrowed your favorite book a few weeks ago and hasn't returned it. You keep your books in good shape and are concerned that it may get tattered by your friend. In this situation you would . . .

- ask to get your book back immediately with no explanation
- ask to borrow something that your friend has and keep it until you get your book
- ask your friend if she is enjoying the book and when she thinks she'll return it

Situation 3

Two weeks ago your mom told you that she would raise your allowance after she saw that you were consistently keeping your room clean. You've made extra effort recently to make sure your room is neat because you're ready for the allowance raise. In this situation you would . . .

- ask Mom if she had an idea of how long it would take to prove to her that you are making more effort to keep your room looking neat
- demand that she give you your allowance raise since your room was looking so neat
- stop cleaning your room since it will take too long for Mom to notice improvement

Perseverance

Persevere by Having a Positive Attitude

Objective: Students will learn that a positive attitude will help you accomplish your goals.

**MONDAY
Check It Out!**

Read or tell the story of "The Little Engine That Could."

Discussion Questions:
1. Why do you think the engine kept trying even though the task was difficult?
2. What does it mean to have an "I Can" attitude?
3. What usually happens when you think you can't do something?
4. What is something you have accomplished by believing that you could do it?
5. How can you encourage yourself when you're given a tough situation or task?

**TUESDAY
Try It Out!**

Have students brainstorm a list of positive, encouraging words and phrases. Then, have each student write a letter to another student in class. In the letters, students should point out special things about their classmates, use encouraging words and phrases, and remind them how it helps to be positive. Have students exchange letters. Encourage students to place these letters in special places to read when they are having trouble being positive about something.

**WEDNESDAY
Take It Out!**

Have the class brainstorm common obstacles that they might encounter when trying to achieve goals in school. For each obstacle, have the students suggest ways to overcome it. Emphasize that a key to overcoming obstacles and dealing with difficulty is attitude.

For example:
1. getting B's on spelling tests no matter how hard you try to get an A
2. not doing well in a certain playground sport or game

Take-Home Activity: Have students ask their parents to help them come up with suggestions for overcoming obstacles that they are currently facing.

**THURSDAY
Talk It Out!**

During group time, have each student share his suggestion for overcoming personal obstacles.

**FRIDAY
Act It Out!**

Have students brainstorm negative phrases that they have heard. Together, rewrite the phrases so that they convey a positive outlook. Post the positive phrases so that students are reminded of the power of positive thinking.

Sample Negative Phrases:
1. I can't do it.
2. It is impossible!
3. This is the end of the world.
4. I'll never be able to do that.
5. That will take forever.

End the activity by singing "If You Have Character and You Know It."

Daily Character Education • CD-0066 • © Carson-Dellosa

Perseverance

Persevere by Balancing Work and Play

Objective: Students will learn they should make time for both work and play.

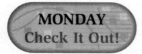

MONDAY
Check It Out!

Read aloud the fable "The Ants and the Grasshopper."

One autumn day, a colony of ants were busy drying grain that they had collected in the summertime. A hungry grasshopper came along and begged the ants for some grain.

One ant asked, "Why did you not store up food during the summer?"

The grasshopper replied, "I passed my summer days with singing."

Another ant said, "Well, if you're foolish enough to only sing all summer, then you shall dance supperless to bed this winter." —Aesop

Discussion Questions:
1. Were the ants fair to the grasshopper?
2. Should students be given time to play?
3. Should students have any chores around the house?
4. How does it feel when you complete a task for someone?
5. Is it important to have time for both having fun and working?

TUESDAY
Try It Out!

Discuss with students the amount of time they spend working (including schoolwork) and playing. After the discussion, ask them if they think that they balance their life with work and play.

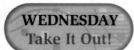

WEDNESDAY
Take It Out!

Provide each student with a copy of "Balancing Work and Play." (See page 42.) Invite each student to picture what happens in her average day. Then, review the directions with students.

Take-Home Activity: Have students complete "Balancing Work and Play" with the help of their parents.

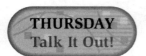

THURSDAY
Talk It Out!

During group time, have students share their completed "Balancing Work and Play" worksheets.

FRIDAY
Act It Out!

Divide the class into small groups. Have each group write a response to the ants from the perspective of the grasshopper. Explain that both the ants and the grasshopper must learn a lesson about having time for work and play in their lives. Ask students if the grasshopper's reply is convincing enough to warrant receiving grain.

End the activity by singing "If You Have Character and You Know It."

Balancing Work and Play

Use the color key below to shade in the amount of time you spend doing the activities on an average day. Then, answer the question at the bottom of the page.

Name _____

Key
chores = red
sleep = blue
play for fun = purple
relaxing time = green
other = brown
school or homework = yellow
lessons/practice for sports, music = orange

Do you balance work and play? Explain your answer.

_____

_____

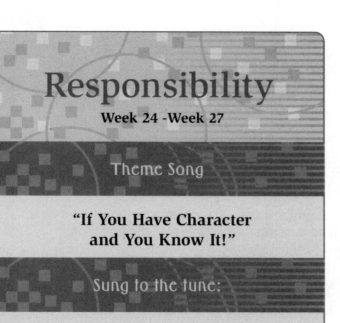

Responsibility
Week 24 -Week 27

Theme Song

"If You Have Character and You Know It!"

Sung to the tune:

"If You're Happy and You Know It"

■ ■ ■ ■ ■ ■ ■

Verse 7:
Be responsible for your actions—
    yes sir-eee!
Be responsible for your actions—
    yes sir-eee!
Learn from each of your mistakes,
You know you have what it takes.
Be responsible for your actions—
    yes sir-eee!

Repeated Verse:
If you have character and you know
    it—let it show!
If you have character and you know
    it—let it show!
In everything along your way,
In all you do and say,
If you have character and you know
    it—let it show!

Dear Parents and Guardians,

For the next four weeks, our class will be exploring ways to demonstrate responsibility. We will be singing our theme song, including the new verse about our actions. Please sing the song at home with your child.

On Wednesdays, look for your child to bring home a question or activity to be completed with your help. The assignments are listed below.

Week One: Your child will ask you to help him or her complete the "If I Were in Charge" worksheet.

Week Two: Your child will ask you to share an example of a mistake that you learned from.

Week Three: Your child will ask you to help make a list of things that he or she can do to calm down when he or she becomes furious.

Week Four: Your child will ask you to share a time when you were disappointed and how you dealt with it.

Responsibility

Be Responsible by Being Accountable

Objective: Students will learn that they are accountable for their actions.

MONDAY
Check It Out!

Read or tell the story of "Rumpelstiltskin."

Discussion Questions:
1. Do you think the miller's daughter meant that promise when she made it?
2. What does it mean to be held accountable for your words or actions?
3. Is it important to keep your promises?
4. Have you ever made a promise that you wish you had not made?
5. Should people be held accountable for their words and actions?

TUESDAY
Try It Out!

Have students brainstorms ways they can demonstrate responsibility. On the board, list their ideas.

For example:
1. When you agree to do something, do it.
2. Be ready to answer for your own actions.
3. Take care of your own matters.
4. Be responsible for things you borrow or use.
5. Think before you act.
6. Don't put things off.

WEDNESDAY
Take It Out!

Discuss with students that like in the story of "Rumpelstiltskin," there are consequences when people don't follow through with their words or actions. Provide students with copies of "If I Were in Charge." (See page 45.)

Take-Home Activity: Have each student complete the "If I Were in Charge" worksheet with his parents.

THURSDAY
Talk It Out!

During group time, have students share their responses to the "If I Were in Charge" worksheet.

FRIDAY
Act It Out!

Divide the class into pairs. Each pair's task is to think of a new version of the scene in "Rumpelstiltskin" in which the miller's daughter promises to give Rumpelstiltskin her first child. The goal is to think of a way to convince Rumpelstiltskin to spin the gold without promising such a great sacrifice.

End the activity by singing "If You Have Character and You Know It."

If I Were in Charge

Pretend that you are the principal of the school. Write the consequences for not following school expectations or breaking the school rules below.

Name _____

1. fighting on the playground

_____

2. stealing money from a student's backpack

_____

3. pushing someone in the bus line

_____

4. talking rudely to a teacher

_____

5. cheating on a test

_____

6. throwing food in the cafeteria

_____

7. being over ten minutes tardy to school more than three times

_____

Responsibility

Be Responsible by Learning from Mistakes

Objective: Students will learn that mistakes provide opportunities for learning and growth.

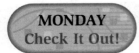

MONDAY
Check It Out!

Read aloud the book *Beverly Billingsly Borrows a Book* by Alexander Stadler (Silver Whistle, 2002). A girl gets her first library card and must learn to accept responsibility for returning an overdue book.

Discussion Questions:
1. Was the consequence for returning the late book as harsh as Beverly thought it would be?
2. Do you think Beverly will return books late again?
3. Can you think of a time when you made a mistake but learned from it?
4. What do think is meant by the expression "You live and you learn"?
5. Why is it important to learn from mistakes?

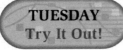

TUESDAY
Try It Out!

Divide the class into small groups. Provide each group with a jigsaw puzzle to complete. Have groups time how long it takes to put them together. Allow groups a second chance to assemble the puzzles and time themselves again. Point out how something can be done more quickly the second time because we learn from our mistakes and are able to avoid them more easily.

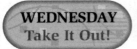

WEDNESDAY
Take It Out!

Share a time when you made a mistake but learned a valuable lesson from it.

Take-Home Activity: Have each student ask her parents for an example of a mistake that they learned from and are willing to share.

THURSDAY
Talk It Out!

During group time, have students share the examples they heard from their parents. This will help reinforce that we all make mistakes—even adults—and the important thing is how we learn from them.

FRIDAY
Act It Out!

Have students brainstorm a list of everyday situations in which common mistakes are made. (Encourage students to include ones that they have made.) For example, taking a test too quickly or not paying attention to instructions. Have students share suggestions for avoiding each mistake.

End the activity by singing "If You Have Character and You Know It."

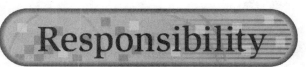

Responsibility

Be Responsible by Dealing with Your Anger

Objective: Students will learn strategies to control anger.

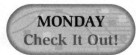

MONDAY
Check It Out!

Read aloud the book *Mean Soup* by Betsy Everitt (Voyager, 1995). A boy is very angry until his mom makes him a special pot of soup.

Discussion Questions:
1. How do you think the boy's mom knows how to help her son?
2. Is it okay to get angry sometimes?
3. What happens when people lose control of their anger?
4. How do people look when they are angry?
5. What are some healthy ways to resolve anger?

TUESDAY
Try It Out!

Explain to students that feeling anger is not wrong. Anger sometimes arises to tell us that what is happening to us doesn't feel good. How we handle or change what is happening is how we demonstrate responsibility for our anger. Figuring out what is causing our anger can help us deal with the feeling. Ask students to share times when they or someone they know made things worse by losing control of anger. Discuss how keeping control could have made things better.

WEDNESDAY
Take It Out!

Teach students how to relax and calm down when they get angry with three C.A.T. steps.
1. **C**alm down. Count to yourself, take deep breaths, or walk away until you have calmed down.
2. **A**nnounce what is wrong. Use words to say what you are upset about.
3. **T**ell what you would like to see happen.

Take-Home Activity: Have each student make a list with her parents of things she can do to calm down when she becomes furious.

THURSDAY
Talk It Out!

During group time, have students share the lists they wrote with their parents. Take the best suggestions that appear most often and write them on a piece of chart paper.

FRIDAY
Act It Out!

Teach students strategies to calm themselves.

1. Practice deep breathing and relaxation exercises by having each child take a deep breath while you count to five, then slowly release the breath. Repeat 10 times.
2. Invite your school's physical education teacher to show students how to do simple, relaxing stretches on the floor.
3. Give students time to close their eyes and envision calming scenes.
   - a balloon floating in the sky
   - a flower blooming in a garden
   - the sun rising above a mountain

End the activity by singing "If You Have Character and You Know It."

Responsibility

Be Responsible by Dealing with Disappointment

Objective: Students will learn that they have control of how they deal with disappointment.

MONDAY
Check It Out!

Read aloud the fable "The Fox and the Grapes."
    Once upon a time, a hungry fox was walking through the forest. He came across some clusters of big, ripe grapes hanging high from a vine. The fox tried and tried to jump high enough to grab the grapes. All that long afternoon she used every trick she knew to reach the grapes, but she couldn't. As the sun sank, she finally gave up. The fox decided that she just couldn't reach them. So she turned away, hiding her disappointment and said, "The old grapes were probably sour anyway." —Aesop

Discussion Questions:
1. Do you think the grapes would have really been sour?
2. Is pretending not to be disappointed a good way to deal with disappointment?
3. Have you ever been disappointed?
4. What do you do when you get frustrated with a situation?
5. When things are going badly, what can you do to make yourself feel better?

TUESDAY
Try It Out!

Have students anonymously write examples of times when they were disappointed or felt like they failed. Put the examples into a bag and have each student pick one example and read it aloud. As students pull examples from the bag, have them offer suggestions for dealing with each disappointment. Remind students not to think of themselves as failures because something didn't turn out well. Make it clear that being disappointed when things don't go your way is a normal feeling. It's important to deal with it and go on.

WEDNESDAY
Take It Out!

As a class, brainstorm short sentences or phrases that students can tell themselves when they are disappointed, such as "Next time I bet this will work out better."

Take-Home Activity: Have each student ask his parents for an example of disappointment that they are willing to share and how they dealt with it.

THURSDAY
Talk It Out!

During group time, have students discuss the disappointments that their parents shared with them. On the board, list the general categories of disappointment: self, others, work, uncontrollable circumstances, etc. List each disappointment discussed in a general category.

FRIDAY
Act It Out!

Remind students of the ending line from "The Fox and the Grapes." Ask students for suggestions on how the fox could have ended the fable in a way that shows that although she is disappointed, she can move on.

For example:
1. It's not my fault that the grapes are too high to reach.
2. Usually I don't have a problem getting food, but this was out of my control.

End the activity by singing "If You Have Character and You Know It."

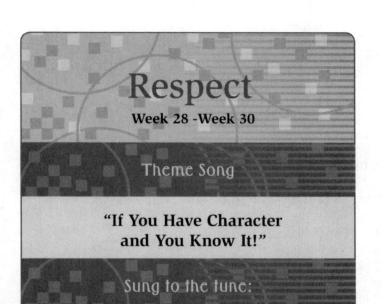

Respect

Week 28 - Week 30

Theme Song

"If You Have Character and You Know It!"

Sung to the tune:

"If You're Happy and You Know It"

■ ■ ■ ■ ■ ■ ■

Verse 8:
Have respect; be considerate—
    yes sir-eee!
Have respect; be considerate—
    yes sir-eee!
Say "you're welcome" and say
    "please,"
Be respectful if you sneeze.
Have respect; be considerate—
    yes sir-eee!

Repeated Verse:
If you have character and you know
    it—let it show!
If you have character and you know
    it—let it show!
In everything along your way,
In all you do and say,
If you have character and you know
    it—let it show!

Dear Parents and Guardians,

For the next three weeks, our class will be discussing ways to demonstrate respect. We will be singing our theme song, including the new verse about being considerate. Please sing the song at home with your child.

On Wednesdays, look for your child to bring home a question or activity to be completed with your help. The assignments are listed below.

Week One: Your child will ask you what you think is the most important of all good manners.

Week Two: Your child will ask you to help him or her complete the "Thinking of You" worksheet.

Week Three: Your child will ask you to share about the best time and way to ask you for something.

Objective: Students will learn that it is respectful to show good manners.

MONDAY
Check It Out!

Introduce this week's topic by explaining to students that showing respectful behavior is a way of saying, "I care for you." On the other hand, acting disrespectfully can say, "I am more important than you."

Discussion Questions:
1. What does it mean to have good manners?
2. Are you expected to use polite language, such as "please" and "thank-you," in your home?
3. Do you say "excuse me" when you want to get someone's attention?
4. Have you ever eaten with someone who had bad manners? What are some bad table manners?
5. Do you think using good manners is appreciated by others?

TUESDAY
Try It Out!

Have students brainstorm ways to show good manners: polite language, table manners, introductions, etc. Next, have students brainstorm words and phrases to remind them of respectful behavior, such as "May I?," "How are you?," "Nice to meet you," "Pardon me," "Please," etc. Write these words and phrases on sentence strips and display them on a bulletin board titled "Please Use Respectful Language."

WEDNESDAY
Take It Out!

Explain the proper way to introduce others. Show students how to properly shake hands, and what to say when meeting a person for the first time, such as "Nice to meet you." Give students a few minutes to practice introductions with each other.

Take-Home Activity: Have students ask parents what they think is the most important of all good manners.

THURSDAY
Talk It Out!

During group time, have students share what their parents said was the most important of all good manners.

FRIDAY
Act It Out!

Announce to students that you will give them time to practice their good manners. Invite a few adult guests into the classroom, such as the principal and media specialist. Give students an opportunity to properly introduce themselves to the adults. Then, provide simple snacks for students and adults to eat to practice good table manners. After your adult guests leave, discuss the good manners that were shown.

End the activity by singing "If You Have Character and You Know It."

Respect

Be Respectful by Considering the Feelings of Others

Objective: Students will learn that it is important to think about other people's feelings.

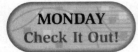

MONDAY
Check It Out!

Read aloud the book *Let's Be Enemies* by Janice May Udry (HarperTrophy, 1988). Two best friends must learn to consider each other.

Discussion Questions:
1. What does it take for the two boys to become friends again?
2. Do you ever have disagreements with your friends?
3. Have you ever hurt someone's feelings?
4. Is it hard to think about other people's feelings?
5. Why is showing respect for other people's feelings important?

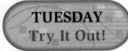

TUESDAY
Try It Out!

Play the game "Your Feelings Count, Too." Give students a situation and have them give thumbs-up or thumbs-down signs, depending upon whether it shows someone being respectful or not. Try to incorporate troublesome behaviors that you see in class.

For example:
1. laughing when someone is telling you something serious
2. listening to a friend when they are sad

WEDNESDAY
Take It Out!

Provide each student with a copy of "Thinking of You" worksheet. (See page 52.) Invite each student to think of a person who she feels she should be more considerate of (a sibling, a parent, a classmate, etc.).

Take-Home Activity: Have students complete the "Thinking of You" worksheets with their parents.

THURSDAY
Talk It Out!

During group time, have students share their "Thinking of You" plans.

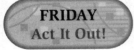

FRIDAY
Act It Out!

Have three student volunteers role-play siblings that are playing a board game. The oldest sibling is winning the game and is smiling and laughing. The youngest sibling is losing and is starting to get upset. The middle sibling is watching the two others and decides to step in so that all three feel good about the game.

End the activity by singing "If You Have Character and You Know It."

Thinking of You

Think about a person who you should be more considerate towards. Then, complete the following information.

Name _____

One person that I would like to be more considerate towards is _____

I can do this by . . .

_____

_____

_____

_____

_____

_____

_____

_____

_____

I'll ask _____ to remind me to use respectful behavior.

Signed _____ Date _____

Respect

Be Respectful by Expressing Wishes—Not Demanding Them

Objective: Students will learn to use appropriate language to express their needs.

**MONDAY
Check It Out!**

Read aloud the fable "The Sun and the Wind."

Once upon a time, long ago, Wind and Sun had an argument about which was the most powerful. To solve the dispute, Sun suggested that they have a contest. The one who could strip a traveler of his cloak the quickest would be the winner and declared the strongest in the universe. Agreeing to the contest, Wind took the first turn. He blew and blew with all his might.

The harder his blasts, the closer the traveler wrapped his cloak around him, but Wind didn't give up. He blew harder until he had no breath left. "Okay," huffed Wind, "let us see if you can do better."

Sun smiled brightly and shone out with all his warmth. The traveler felt the hot rays and began taking off his cloak. So, Sun was victorious. —Aesop

Discussion Questions:
1. How was Sun's approach different than Wind's?
2. Why do you think Sun's calm approach worked?
3. Have you ever tried to make someone do something?
4. Are crying, pouting, or nagging convincing ways to get what you want?
5. If you were a parent, would you be frustrated if your child threw tantrums to try to get what he wanted?

**TUESDAY
Try It Out!**

As a class, write a song to remind students how to appropriately express their wishes. Put the words to a familiar tune.

For example: (to the tune of "Row, Row, Row Your Boat")
Cry, whine, beg, and squeal
Won't get you what you need.
Ask it in a respectful way.
With that you will succeed.

**WEDNESDAY
Take It Out!**

Read the phrase "You can catch more flies with honey than with vinegar." Ask students to write what they think the phrase means. Collect the students' responses and read them aloud. Then, explain the true meaning of the phrase.

Take-Home Activity: Have students ask their parents the best time and way to ask for something that they really want.

**THURSDAY
Talk It Out!**

During group time, have students share the ways parents suggested to ask for things.

**FRIDAY
Act It Out!**

Divide the class into pairs. Each pair's task is to role-play a student asking her parent for something she really wants. Remind students to use the suggestions given by their parents.

End the activity by singing "If You Have Character and You Know It."

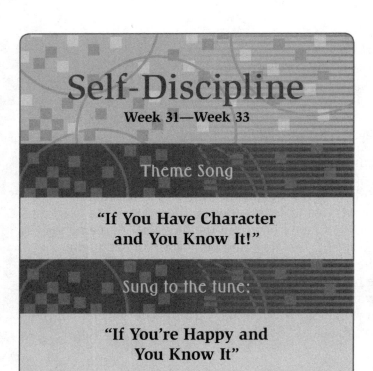

Self-Discipline

Week 31—Week 33

Theme Song

"If You Have Character and You Know It!"

Sung to the tune:

"If You're Happy and You Know It"

■ ■ ■ ■ ■ ■ ■

Verse 9:
Self-discipline makes you stronger—
   yes sir-eee!
Self-discipline makes you stronger—
   yes sir-eee!
If you always do your share,
You'll earn friends everywhere.
Self-discipline makes you stronger—
   yes sir-eee!

Repeated Verse:
If you have character and you know
   it—let it show!
If you have character and you know
   it—let it show!
In everything along your way,
In all you do and say,
If you have character and you know
   it—let it show!

Dear Parents and Guardians,

For the next three weeks, our class will be working on ways to demonstrate self-discipline. We will be singing our theme song, including the new verse about making yourself stronger. Please sing the song at home with your child.

On Wednesdays, look for your child to bring home a question or activity to be completed with your help. The assignments are listed below.

Week One: Your child will ask you if he or she can take on a new household task or responsibility.

Week Two: Your child will share his or her "I Can Change Me" plan and ask for your advice about accomplishing a goal.

Week Three: Please help your child memorize a question that he or she could ask to consider consequences of certain actions.

Self-Discipline

Be Self-Disciplined by Doing Your Share

Objective: Students will learn that they should take part in daily tasks.

MONDAY
Check It Out!

Read aloud the book *Clean Your Room, Harvey Moon!* by Pat Cummings (Scott Foresman, 1994). A boy learns that sometimes moms have different ideas about what is clean.

Discussion Questions:
1. How would you describe Harvey?
2. Do you think you are old enough to have responsibilities around your home?
3. What kinds of chores are you expected to do?
4. Do you usually have to be reminded to do your household responsibilities?
5. Should everyone in a household be required to contribute to chores?

TUESDAY
Try It Out!

Give students a situation which involves personal responsibility and self-discipline. Have them write what they would do in response.

For example:
It is Saturday, your mom is at work, and your dad is in the garage working on a project. Your mom left you a note instructing you to eat a bowl of cereal, then clean your room immediately. You just remembered that your favorite TV show is on. What should you do?

WEDNESDAY
Take It Out!

Ask students to think about the tasks that their parents do around their homes. Invite each student to think of an appropriate, additional task that she could begin helping with.

Take-Home Activity: Have students ask their parents if they can take on or help with additional household tasks.

THURSDAY
Talk It Out!

During group time, have students share their parents' responses to offering extra help around their homes.

FRIDAY
Act It Out!

Have students role-play the situation presented in class on Tuesday. Have a small group role-play an example showing poor self-discipline and have the next group role-play the situation showing excellent self-discipline. Explain to students that self-discipline is a skill that must be practiced.

End the activity by singing "If You Have Character and You Know It."

Self-Discipline

Be Self-Disciplined by Changing Bad Habits

Objective: Students will learn strategies to break bad habits.

MONDAY
Check It Out!

Read aloud the book *Mrs. Piggle-Wiggle* by Betty MacDonald (HarperTrophy, 1985). A woman helps students cure their bad habits.

Discussion Questions:
1. How was Mrs. Piggle-Wiggle able to help others with their bad habits?
2. What are some common bad habits?
3. Do you have any bad habits?
4. Are there any of your bad habits that you would like to break?
5. Why is it sometimes difficult to break bad habits?

TUESDAY
Try It Out!

Have each student think of one habit or area of his life he would like to improve. Provide each student with a copy of "I Can Change Me." (See page 57.) With this, students will write plans to change or get rid of bad habits. Explain to students that the behaviors they choose must be behaviors they are willing to work on. Have students complete the first line of the plan. Collect the plans.

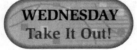
WEDNESDAY
Take It Out!

Return the "I Can Change Me" plans. Have students complete them in class.

Take-Home Activity: Have students share their "I Can Change Me" plans with their parents. Then, have students ask their parents' advice for accomplishing their goals.

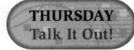
THURSDAY
Talk It Out!

During group time, have students share their parents' advice for accomplishing their goals.

FRIDAY
Act It Out!

Have students brainstorm positive words and phrases to encourage each other as they try to break their bad habits. Provide students with craft materials to write the words and phrases on poster board cut into triangle pennant shapes. Display them around the classroom.

End the activity by singing "If You Have Character and You Know It."

 Daily Character Education • CD-0066 • © Carson-Dellosa

I Can Change Me

Think about an area in your life that you would like to improve. Set a goal for yourself. Then, complete the following information.

Name _____

One thing I would like to change about me is _____

I can achieve this by _____

_____

_____

To help me, I will ask _____ to ask me about my progress.

My goal is to _____

I would like to achieve my goal by (date) _____

Signed _____

Today's date _____

Witness _____

Objective: Students will learn the importance of thinking before they act.

**MONDAY
Check It Out!**

Read aloud the fable "The Two Frogs."

Once upon a time, two frogs lived in a shallow pond. As summer wore on, it was hot and dry, and the pond dried up. The frogs left to find another watery home. After hopping most of a summer day, they came to a well that appeared to be full of water. One frog quickly said, "Let's jump in and live in this well. It will furnish us with shelter, water, and food."

The other frog thought and said, "That might be a good plan now, but when the well dries up, how would we get out again from so deep a dry well?" —Aesop

Discussion Questions:
1. Which of the two frogs thought the situation through?
2. Did the first frog consider what could happen?
3. When have you done something without considering the consequences?
4. What often happens when someone doesn't think before he acts?
5. How can you improve your ability to consider consequences?

**TUESDAY
Try It Out!**

As a class, write a song to remind students how to consider the consequences of their actions. Put the words to a familiar tune.

For example: (to the tune of "You Are My Sunshine")
I must think before I act.
I must know that it is right.
It is important
to consider my actions.
It will help to make my future bright.

**WEDNESDAY
Take It Out!**

Invite each student to select a question in order to help her when put in a situation where consequences should be considered.
For example:
1. Would I be breaking a family rule?
2. Will I be happy with myself if I do this?

Take-Home Activity: Have students share the questions they selected with their parents so that they can memorize their questions.

**THURSDAY
Talk It Out!**

Explain to students that some actions (such as smoking or stealing) can result in very serious consequences. Tell students how important it is to practice considering consequences. That way, they'll be better prepared to handle tougher decisions later.

**FRIDAY
Act It Out!**

Divide the class into pairs. Have each pair practice saying their selected questions with each other. After practicing, allow each student a chance to recite his question to the class.

End the activity by singing "If You Have Character and You Know It."

Trustworthiness

Week 34 -Week 36

"If You Have Character and You Know It!"

Sung to the tune:

"If You're Happy and You Know It"

■ ■ ■ ■ ■ ■ ■

Verse 10:
Be trustworthy; be true-blue—
    yes sir-eee!
Be trustworthy; be true-blue—
    yes sir-eee!
Keep the promises you make.
Your good word is at stake.
Be trustworthy; be true-blue—
    yes sir-eee!

Repeated Verse:
If you have character and you know
    it—let it show!
If you have character and you know
    it—let it show!
In everything along your way,
In all you do and say,
If you have character and you know
    it—let it show!

Dear Parents and Guardians,

For the next three weeks, our class will be exploring ways to demonstrate trustworthiness. We will be singing our theme song, including the new verse about being true-blue. Please sing the song at home with your child.

On Wednesdays, look for your child to bring home a question or activity to be completed with your help. The assignments are listed below.

Week One: Your child will ask you to name a person that you consider to be trustworthy.

Week Two: Your child will ask you if someone has ever tried to take advantage of you. He or she will also ask for your advice on not being taken advantage of.

Week Three: Your child will ask if you would rather be told of something bad immediately after it happens, or if you would rather wait until time has passed and find out about it later.

Trustworthiness

Be Trustworthy by Keeping Your Word

Objective: Students will learn that their word should be valued and held in respect.

MONDAY
Check It Out!

Read aloud the book *Kirsten's Promise* by Janet Beeler Shaw (Pleasant Company Publications, 2003). A girl makes a promise but realizes that there are a few times when you must break your word.

Discussion Questions:
1. What would you have done in the girl's place?
2. Has a friend ever asked you to keep a secret?
3. Have you ever told someone you would do something and didn't?
4. When you give your word to someone, why is it important to keep it?
5. Are there times when you must break your word?

TUESDAY
Try It Out!

Explain to students that it is important to be known as a person who keeps his word. Have students brainstorm a list of people or groups of people known for being trustworthy. After students give suggestions, have them look for things those people have in common in addition to their trustworthiness.

WEDNESDAY
Take It Out!

Explain to students what a contract is (a written agreement that lists the details agreed upon.) Have the class create a contract to help each other keep their word. Provide students with a piece of chart paper. Then, have students sign the agreement signifying that they promise to keep the contract.

Take-Home Activity: Have each student ask her parents to name a person that they think is trustworthy.

THURSDAY
Talk It Out!

During group time, have students share the names of the people their parents said were trustworthy. See how many of the names match the list that students made on Tuesday.

FRIDAY
Act It Out!

Divide the class into pairs. Give students time to share secrets or make promises to each other. Remind students that being trustworthy will make them valued as friends.

End the activity by singing "If You Have Character and You Know It."

Be Trustworthy by Not Taking Advantage of Others

Objective: Students will learn that it is dishonest to take advantage of others.

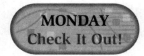

MONDAY
Check It Out!

Read aloud the fable "The Blind Woman and the Physician."

Once upon a time, there was a blind woman. She offered a deal to a physician. If he could cure her blindness, he would receive a large sum of money from her. If she remained blind, he would receive no money. For months he applied salve to her eyes, and as he left her home, he stole something from her. Eventually, he took everything in her house. By the time the physician had taken everything the woman owned, he had healed her. He demanded the promised payment. The woman looked around her home and saw none of her things. She told the physician that she would not pay him. The physician insisted on payment, and when the woman refused to pay, she was called before the town judge.

In court, the woman stated, "I did promise to give him money, if he could give me my sight. Now he declares that I am healed. I feel that I am still blind. Before I became blind, I saw many valuable goods in my house. Though the physician says I am cured of my blindness, I am not able to see anything in my house." —Aesop

Discussion Questions:
1. Do you think that the woman owes the physician anything?
2. Have you ever felt taken advantage of?
3. Why is it wrong to take advantage of others?
4. Would you consider someone who takes advantage of others trustworthy?
5. How can you avoid taking advantage of other people?

TUESDAY
Try It Out!

To build trust in students, assign partners. Give each pair a piece of long, clean, dark cloth. Have one member of each pair wear the cloth as a blindfold. Then, have her partner carefully guide her around a safe, open area outside. After each has had a turn at being blindfolded, discuss the level of trust it takes. Explain that friends and family need to have enough trust in each other that they don't doubt or question each other.

WEDNESDAY
Take It Out!

Have students think of popular stories in which a character was taken advantage of, such as "Cinderella" and "Pinnochio." Discuss how those characters, who were often kind and trusting, are rewarded in the end for their good character.

Take-Home Activity: Have each student ask his parents if someone has tried to take advantage of them and share advice about how not to be taken advantage of.

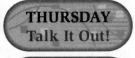

THURSDAY
Talk It Out!

During group time, have students share their parents' advice about how not to be taken advantage of.

FRIDAY
Act It Out!

Divide the class into groups of three. Give each student a lunch bag and markers. Allow each group member to select a character from Monday's fable, and have him decorate his bag to look like the blind woman, the physician, or the judge. Allow students to retell the fable using the puppets.

End the activity by singing "If You Have Character and You Know It."

Trustworthiness

Be Trustworthy by Not Trying to Cover Up

Objective: Students will learn to be honest when accidents happen.

**MONDAY
Check It Out!**

Read aloud the book *It Wasn't My Fault* by Helen Lester (Houghton Mifflin, 1989). An accident-prone boy tries to find someone to blame.

Discussion Questions:
1. Was the bird laying an egg on the boy's head his fault?
2. Have you ever accidentally done something and then tried to cover it up?
3. Do problems usually get better or worse if you try to cover them up?
4. When the truth comes out after a cover-up, can trust be lost?
5. What is the best thing to do when you have an accident?

**TUESDAY
Try It Out!**

Ask students, "When there is an accident, instead of trying to cover up, what can be done?" Have students brainstorm a list of responses. List them on the board.

For example:
1. Think about the facts of what happened.
2. Tell the truth.
3. Get ready for the consequences.
4. Be proud of your honesty.

**WEDNESDAY
Take It Out!**

Have each student share an example of when he has tried to cover up something.

Take-Home Activity: Have each student ask her parents if they would rather be told about something bad immediately after it happens, or if they would rather wait until time has passed and find out about it later.

**THURSDAY
Talk It Out!**

During group time, have students share their parents' answers to last night's question. Since the majority of parents will probably answer that they would rather know immediately, point out to students that the earlier the truth comes out, the quicker everyone can get past it.

**FRIDAY
Act It Out!**

On the floor, lay out a full-sized, plain flat sheet. Allow students to take turns placing their hands into child-safe paint and then making handprints on the sheet. After all students have put their handprints on the sheet, title it "Hand It to Us for Being Trustworthy!" Display the sheet in the classroom.

End the activity by singing "If You Have Character and You Know It."

Children's Book List

Beverly Billingsly Borrows a Book by Alexander Stadler (Silver Whistle, 2002).

Clean Your Room, Harvey Moon! by Pat Cummings (Scott Foresman, 1994).

Doctor De Soto by William Steig (Sunburst, 1990).

The Giving Tree by Shel Silverstein (HarperCollins Juvenile Books, 1964).

It Wasn't My Fault by Helen Lester (Houghton Mifflin, 1989).

Junie B., First Grader: Cheater Pants by Barbara Park (Random House, 2003).

Kirsten's Promise by Janet Beeler Shaw (Pleasant Company Publications, 2003).

Let's Be Enemies by Janice May Udry (HarperTrophy, 1988).

Mean Soup by Betsy Everitt (Voyager, 1995).

Moose, of Course! by Lynn Plourde (Down East Books, 1999).

Mr. Lincoln's Way by Patricia Polacco (Philomel, 2001).

Mrs. Piggle-Wiggle by Betty MacDonald (HarperTrophy, 1985).

The Rag Coat by Lauren A. Mills (Little, Brown & Co., 1991).

The Real Thief by William Steig (Farrar, Straus and Giroux, 1985).

The Recess Queen by Alexis O'Neill (Scholastic, 2002).

We the Kids: The Preamble to the Constitution of the United States by David Catrow (Dial Books for Young Readers, 2002).

Why Are You Fighting, Davy? by Brigitte Weninger (North South Books, 1999).

Wombat Divine by Mem Fox (Voyager, 1999).

Theme Song, "If You Have Character and You Know It!"
Sung to the tune: "If You're Happy and You Know It"

If you have character and you know it—let it show!
If you have character and you know it—let it show!
In everything along your way,
In all you do and say,
If you have character and you know it—let it show!
(repeated opening verse)

A good citizen loves the earth—yes sir-eee!
A good citizen loves the earth—yes sir-eee!
Take care of everything that breathes,
People, pets, and even trees,
A good citizen loves the earth—yes sir-eee!

Be compassionate and kind—yes sir-eee!
Be compassionate and kind—yes sir-eee!
If you care and do things right,
You'll sleep better through the night.
Be compassionate and kind—yes sir-eee!

Be fair with a peaceful heart—yes sir-eee!
Be fair with a peaceful heart—yes sir-eee!
If you play by every rule,
Working with others can be cool.
Be fair with a peaceful heart—yes sir-eee!

Be honest; tell the truth—yes sir-eee!
Be honest; tell the truth—yes sir-eee!
If you don't steal, cheat, or lie,
You won't need an alibi.
Be honest; tell the truth—yes sir-eee!

Have integrity; do your best—yes sir-eee!
Have integrity; do your best—yes sir-eee!
And deep down in your heart,
You will always do your part.
Have integrity; do your best—yes sir-eee!

Persevere by sticking to it—yes sir-eee!
Persevere by sticking to it—yes sir-eee!
If you're patient and you try,
Your only limit is the sky.
Persevere by sticking to it—yes sir-eee!

Be responsible for your actions—yes sir-eee!
Be responsible for your actions—yes sir-eee!
Learn from each of your mistakes.
You know you have what it takes.
Be responsible for your actions—yes sir-eee!

Have respect; be considerate—yes sir-eee!
Have respect; be considerate—yes sir-eee!
Say "you're welcome" and say "please,"
Be respectful if you sneeze.
Have respect; be considerate—yes sir-eee!

Self-discipline makes you stronger—yes sir-eee!
Self-discipline makes you stronger—yes sir-eee!
If you always do your share,
You'll earn friends everywhere.
Self-discipline makes you stronger—yes sir-eee!

Be trustworthy; be true-blue—yes sir-eee!
Be trustworthy; be true-blue—yes sir-eee!
Keep the promises you make.
Your good word is at stake.
Be trustworthy; be true-blue—yes sir-eee!

 Daily Character Education • CD-0066 • © Carson-Dellosa